COLLINS•LONGMAN

Mapstart

Simon Catling

Principal Lecturer in Education, Oxford Polytechnic

Contents

Looking down at everyday objects

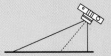

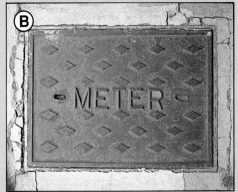
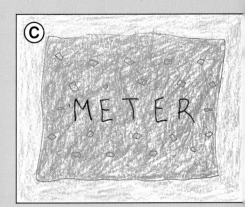

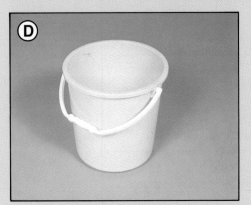
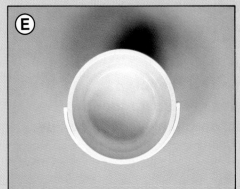
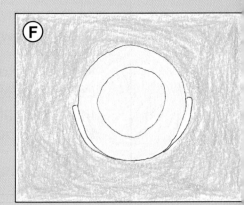

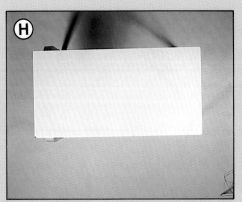
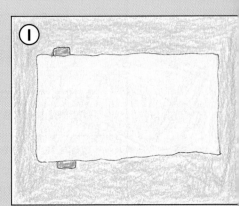

Photos **A**, **D** and **G** show objects you can see every day. The photos were taken **looking down from the side.**

Photos **B**, **E** and **H** were taken **looking down from straight above.** You can see the shape of each object from above.

C, **F** and **I** are **plans** of each object. They show the **shape** of each object looking down from straight above.

1 Name the three objects in **A**, **D** and **G**.
2 What does a plan show?
3 Draw a plan of an object on your table.

J

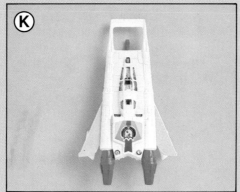

K

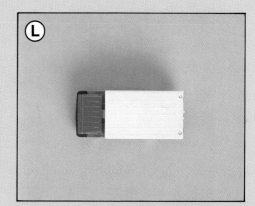

L

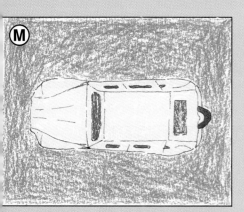

M

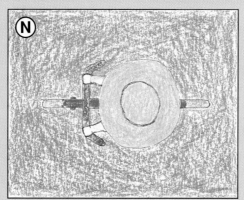

N

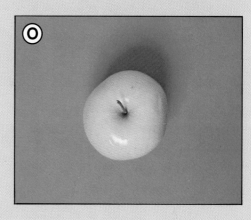

O

P

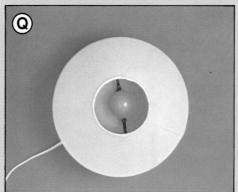

Q

Person on a bike

Car

Lorry

Space shuttle

Apple

Helicopter

Lamp

Telephone

Look at the photos and plans on this page.
They show the **view** looking down from straight above.
The names of each object are in the box.

1 Name the object in each photo.
2 Name the object in each plan.
3 Draw a plan of the object in each photo.
4 Draw plans of some objects in your classroom.

Looking down-around the school

A

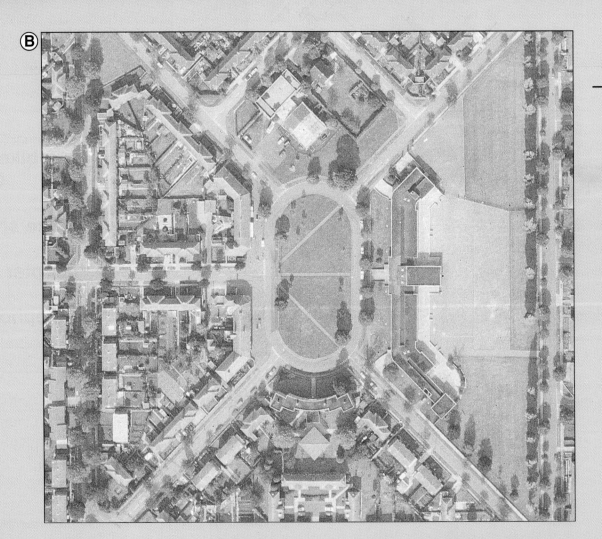

B

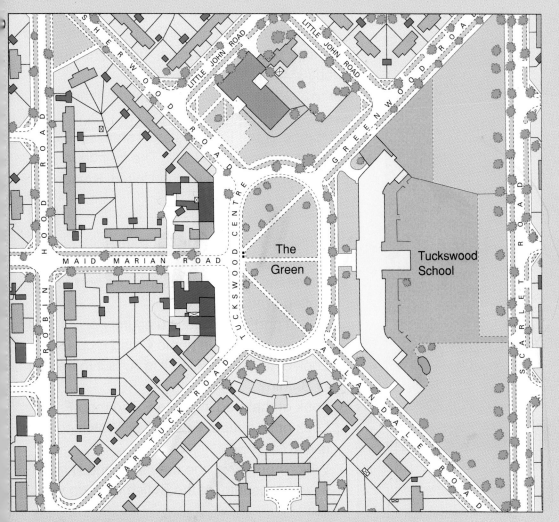

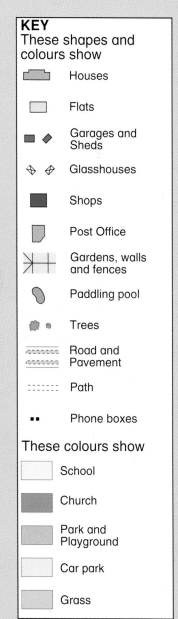

A and **B** are photos of Tuckswood School. They were taken from a plane.

A is an **oblique view** of the school. You are looking down at the back of the school. You can see the school building and the playground. You can see some of the area around the school. At the front of the school you can see The Green and the shops.

In photo **B** you are looking straight down at the school. This is called a **vertical view**.
In the vertical view you can see the shape of the school and some of the roads and buildings near the school.

C is a map of Tuckswood School. It shows the same area that you can see in photo **B**.
Use the **key** to see what the shapes and colours show. The roads are named on the map.

1 Which colour on the map shows the school building?
2 How many roads are named on map **C**?
3 Which other places are named on the map?
4 Which building is the car park next to?
5 What would you walk across to go from the Post Office to the school?
6 Why do you think the road around The Green is called Tuckswood Centre?

Looking down - the view from space

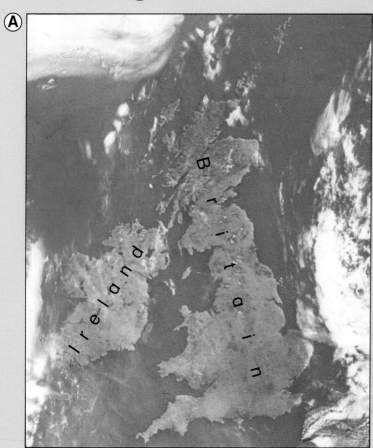

Satellite photo of the British Isles

A is a satellite photo of the British Isles. It shows the shape of the British Isles. There are many islands in the British Isles.
The two largest islands are named on the photo.

B is a map of the British Isles. It shows the countries in the British Isles. The four countries coloured yellow make up the United Kingdom.

?

1 Which are the two largest islands in the British Isles?
2 Name the four countries that are part of the United Kingdom.
3 Which part of Ireland is a country on its own?
4 Look at the area in photo **C** and map **D**. Look at its shape. Find it in **A**. Is it in Ireland or Britain?
5 Look at the area in photo **E** and map **F**. Look at its shape. Find it in **B**. Which country is it in?
6 Which country is the area in **G** and **H** in?
7 In which country of the British Isles do you live?

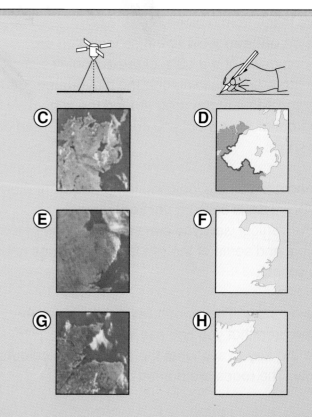

Satellite photo of Europe

I is another photo taken by a satellite. It shows a part of the Earth named Europe. Find Ireland and Britain in the photo. They look small in this photo.

J is a map of the part of Europe you can see in **I**. It shows the land and the sea. Ireland and Britain are part of Europe. There are many other islands that are part of Europe. Find them in **I** and **J**.

K is another photo taken from space. It shows a view of the Earth. Through the clouds you can see the land and sea.

1 What colour is the sea in photos **I** and **K**?
2 Which colour shows the land in **J**?
3 Draw the shape of the largest island in Europe.
4 Draw the shape of two more islands you can see.
5 Find Europe in **K**. Name another large area of land you can see.
6 Look at a globe and find out which parts of the Earth you cannot see in **K**.

Satellite photo of the Earth

What is a plan?

A is a photo of a classroom. You can see most of the room, but not all of it. Look at **B**. It shows how the classroom would look if you could take a photo looking down from straight above. It is a **vertical view** of the classroom.

Find **where** some of the things you can see in photo **A** are in view **B**. Find some objects in **B** that you cannot see in photo **A**.

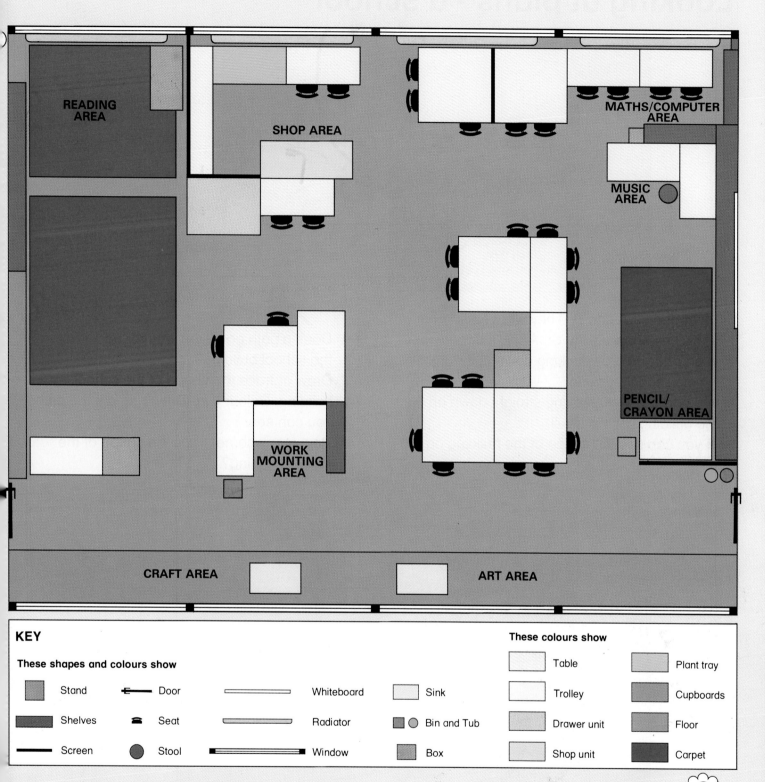

KEY

These shapes and colours show

▭ Stand	⊏ Door	▭ Whiteboard	▭ Sink	
▭ Shelves	☎ Seat	▭ Radiator	◧ ● Bin and Tub	
▬ Screen	● Stool	▭ Window	▭ Box	

These colours show

▭ Table	▭ Plant tray		
▭ Trolley	▭ Cupboards		
▭ Drawer unit	▭ Floor		
▭ Shop unit	▭ Carpet		

C is a plan of the same classroom. It shows the **layout** of the room. You can see where things are. It also shows the shapes of the furniture in the room.

The **key** tells you **what** the shapes and colours mean on the plan.

Some areas in the room have been named.

1 How many seats does plan **C** show?
2 Which colour in the key shows carpets?
3 Name three objects next to the largest carpet.
4 Name three objects you pass on your right going from the shop to the smallest carpet.

9

Looking at plans - a school

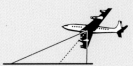

Look at photos **A** and **B**. They were taken from a plane. They show part of St. Alban's School.
A is an **oblique view** looking down at the front of the main school building.
B is a **vertical view** looking straight down on the same building.
In **B** you can see the shape of the building on the ground.

1 Does a path go all the way round the school building?
2 Draw or trace the shape of the school building. Colour it in. Draw round it the paths you can see.
3 How many corners has the shape of the school building?

Ⓑ

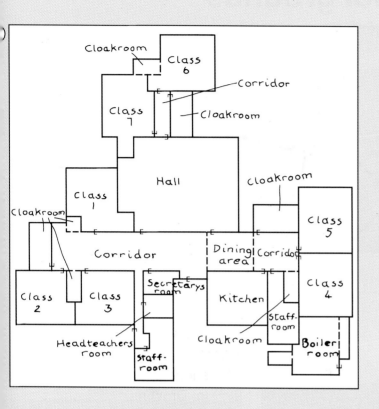

Photos **A** and **B** show you the outside of St. Alban's School.
C is a plan of the inside of the school. It shows where all the rooms are in the school.

Plan **C** was used to make a **survey** of the rooms. It is a **base plan**. It shows only the rooms.
The survey was about what the rooms in the main school building are used for.
What each room is used for was written on the base plan.

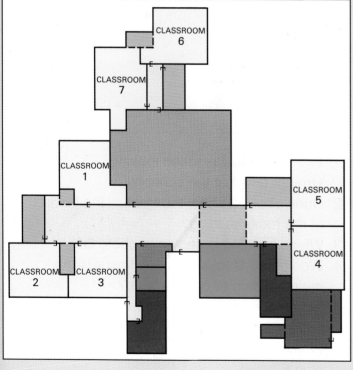

Plan **D** was made after the survey. It has been coloured in to show what each of the rooms is used for.
Some of the rooms have been numbered.
Use the **key** to help you see what each colour shows.

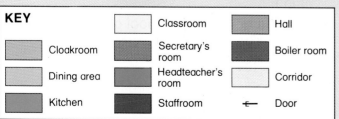

KEY

			Classroom		Hall
	Cloakroom		Secretary's room		Boiler room
	Dining area		Headteacher's room		Corridor
	Kitchen		Staffroom	←	Door

1 How were the classrooms shown on the survey plan?
2 Which colour shows the hall on plan **D**?
3 What does yellow show on plan **D**?
4 Which rooms are next to the headteacher's room?
5 How many rooms are next to the hall?
6 Which two rooms are furthest apart in the main building?
7 Which rooms do you pass on your right going from classroom 2 to classroom 4?
8 Why do you think the classrooms are numbered on the plans?

11

Looking at plans - school grounds

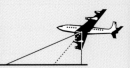

Photo **A** shows the buildings, playground and playing field of St. Alban's School. It is an oblique view of the school.

Photos **B**, **C** and **D** were taken on the ground. Photo **B** shows the way into the school. Look carefully at **C** and **D** to see which parts of the school they show.

Photo **E** is a vertical view of the school grounds. The parts of the school have been named. Find them on photo **A**.

F is a plan of the school grounds. It was made after a survey of the use of the school grounds. Colours have been used to show the different parts of the school. The key shows what the colours mean. The plan also shows the rooms inside the school buildings.

1 Which photo was taken looking straight down at the school?
2 Does photo **C** show the front or the back of the main building?
3 Which building is shown in photo **D**?
4 Was photo **D** taken looking towards the main building or away from it?
5 Which parts of the school are named in photo **E**?
6 Which colour shows the playing field in plan **F**?
7 Find the trees in the school grounds. Which part of the main building are they nearest to?
8 How many paths lead from the buildings to the playground?

12

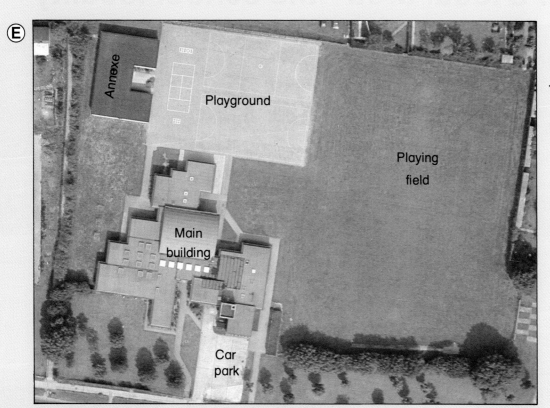

E

Annexe

Playground

Playing
field

Main
building

Car
park

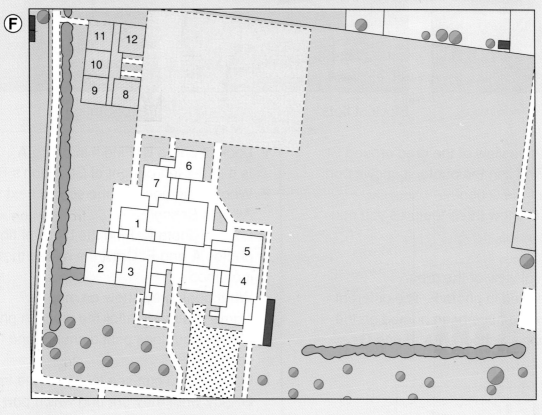

F

11 12

10

9 8

6

7

1

2 3

5

4

KEY

	Main building		Car park		Shed		Fence
	Annexe		Garden		Hedge		Path
	Playground		Grass		Trees		

Maps of a local area - the school locality

(A)

(B) Church

(C) Block of flats

(D) Petrol Station

Photo **A** is an oblique view of the area around St. Alban's School. Find it in the photo. It shows part of the local area of the school.
Photos **B**, **C** and **D** show three features you can see in **A**.

Photo **F** is a vertical view of the area.
G is a **map** of the area in photo **F**. The different parts of the local area have been named on the map. Find St. Alban's School on **A**, **F** and **G**.

(E)

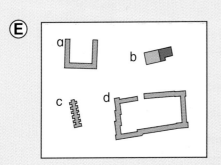

1 Look at photo **B**. Find it in photo **A**. Is it to the left or right of St. Alban's School?
2 What is the name of the school next to St. Alban's School?
3 Look at photo **C**. Find the block of flats in photos **A** and **F**. Draw the shape that shows it on map **G**.
4 What does grey show on map **G**.?
5 Name two roads near the place in photo **D**.
6 Which road goes past a church and two schools?
7 In box **E** you can see four features from map **G**. Say what they are and which part of the local area they are in.
8 If you walked from the roundabout towards Monkswick Road, what would you pass on your right?

(F)

(G)

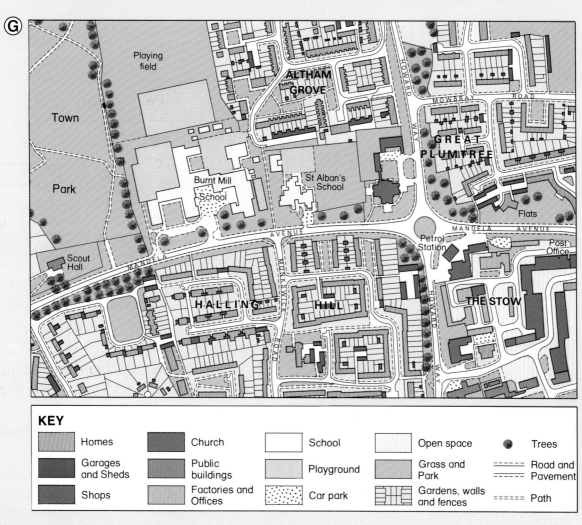

KEY

Homes	Church	School	Open space	● Trees
Garages and Sheds	Public buildings	Playground	Grass and Park	--- Road and Pavement
Shops	Factories and Offices	Car park	Gardens, walls and fences	===== Path

15

Making a map

The new block of flats in **B** has been built near Emma's home in the village of Wheatley. The people who will move into the flats need to know where the local shops are. Emma wanted to make a map to show them the way to the shops from the new flats.

First Emma drew map **A**. She drew it from memory, putting in the shops she remembered that are near to the flats.

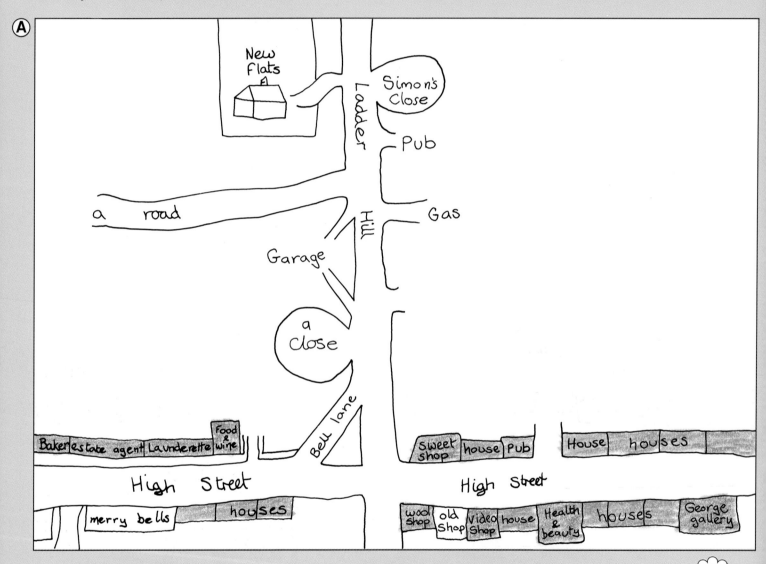

1 Find the new flats on map **A**. Which road are the flats next to?
2 Along which road are the shops?
3 What other places did Emma draw beside the shops?
4 Why would it help someone in the flats to know where the garage is?
5 How many shops does Emma show on Map **A**?

16

When she had finished her map Emma wanted to be sure the map showed all the shops and the route to them. She went out with her map to check that it was accurate.

She found that she had to change some of the places she had drawn so that her map was correct. Then she drew map **C** to show the shops and roads accurately.

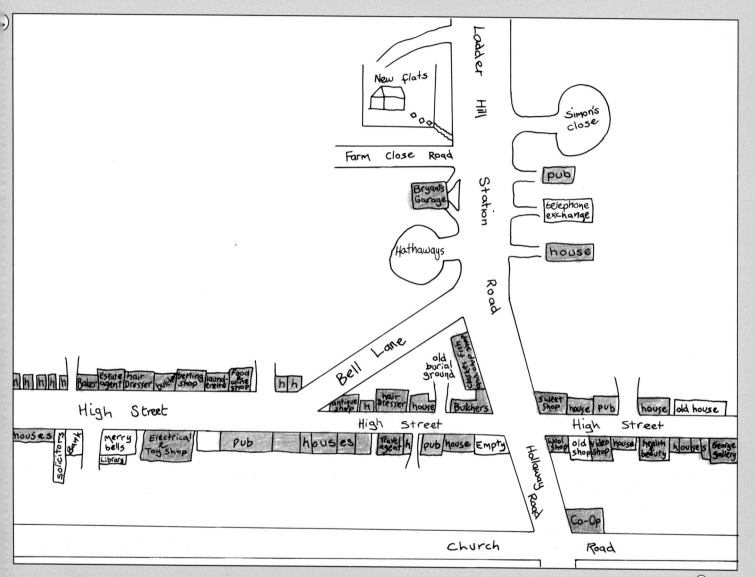

1 Name five shops on map **C** which are not on map **A**.
2 Which roads would you walk along to go from the flats to the baker?
3 List some other changes Emma made to her map when she redrew it.
4 Draw a map to show the way to a place near your home, so that someone else can use it to get there.

Story maps

In the story of **Fantastic Mr. Fox** there are three farmers who Mr. Fox is always stealing food from. The farmers are Farmer Boggis, Farmer Bunce and Farmer Bean.

In **A** you can see the three farms. Farmer Bean lives in a farm which has trees all around it. Find it. Farmer Boggis lives opposite Farmer Bean. Farmer Bunce lives in the farm by the stream.

A

Mr. Fox steals chickens from Farmer Boggis. He takes ducks and geese from Farmer Bunce and he steals turkeys from farmer Bean.

1 Which farm is highest up the side of the valley?
2 Whose farm is in the bottom of the valley?
3 Whose farm is by the large tree on the cliff?
4 Which two farms are on the same side of the stream?
5 Whose farm has an orchard of apple trees?

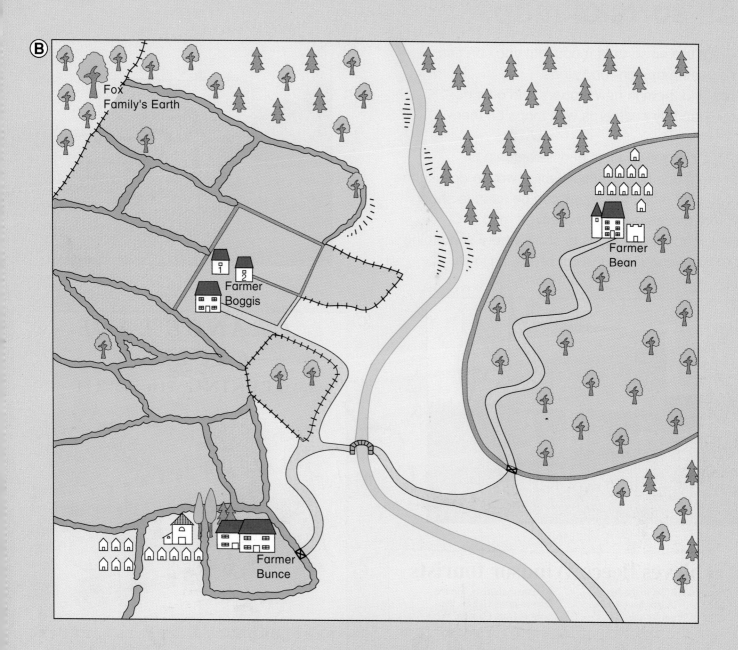

B is a picture map of the area where farmers Bean, Boggis and Bunce live. You can also see where the Fox family live in their earth.

Map **B** shows where the farmers keep their turkeys, chickens and ducks and geese. It shows the fields round the farms. Some of the fields are for grazing and some are ploughed for planting crops like wheat and barley.

1 Which farmer does Mr. Fox live nearest to?
2 Which colour shows fields animals can graze in? Use picture **A** to help you.
3 Find Farmer Bean's turkey houses on map **B**. Are they in front of or behind his farm house?
4 Why can you not see Farmer Bean's turkey houses in picture **A**?
5 Make a key for the map to show what the pictures and colours mean.

All sorts of maps

There are all sorts of maps that you can find.
You see maps on road signs.
You find them in newspapers and adverts.
You can buy postcards with maps on them.

Maps can tell you lots of different things.
Some maps help you see which way to go, like the road sign map in **A**. Maps can be used to show where places are, like the advert map in **C**.
Newspapers use maps to show where something has happened, like the car break-ins in **D**.

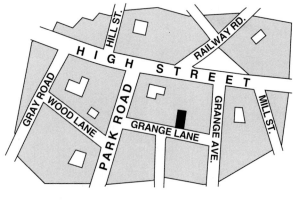

GRANGE LANE CYCLES

OPENING 4th APRIL

BEST PRODUCTS AT BEST PRICES
12 Grange Lane   TEL. 572601
OPEN 9.00-6.00 MON. TILL SAT.

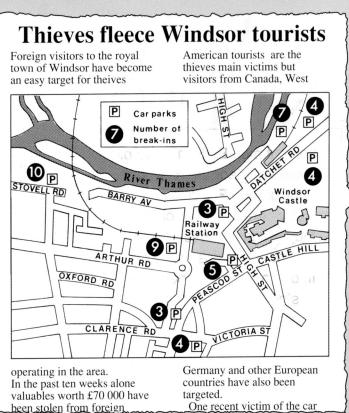

Thieves fleece Windsor tourists

Foreign visitors to the royal town of Windsor have become an easy target for theives

American tourists are the thieves main victims but visitors from Canada, West

operating in the area.
In the past ten weeks alone valuables worth £70 000 have been stolen from foreign

Germany and other European countries have also been targeted.
One recent victim of the car

1 Which map would help someone driving a car?
2 What does the map of the industrial estate show you?
3 Why would an advert like **C** include a map?
4 Look at map **A**. Would you turn left or right to go to Stirling?
5 Use map **D** to write a report for the newspaper about the car break-ins.

20

Maps can tell you about towns you can visit and about different places of interest to visit in a tourist area.

Postcard maps **E** and **F** are often bought and sent by tourists who visit York and the Yorkshire Dales. They show places of historic interest which are visited by tourists.

1 Look at map **E**. Name two places you could visit near the railway station.
2 Look at map **F**. Which places could you visit where there are castles?
3 Maps **E** and **F** have no key. Make a key for one of the postcard maps.
4 Imagine you are sending one of the postcard maps to a friend. Write a message to say which places you visited. Write your friend's address.
5 Make a collection of all sorts of maps. See how many types of maps you can find.

North East South and West

A

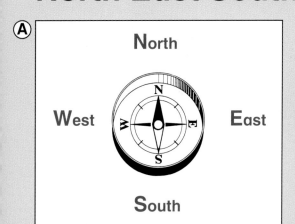

B is a **picture map** of a playground.
Find the pond in the centre of the playground.
Now find the slide.
To say which way it is from the pond to the slide, we can use **compass directions**.
The four points of the compass are **north**, **east**, **south** and **west**.
The **compass** in **A** shows that the slide is **north** of the pond.
Find the letters **N**, **E**, **S** and **W** round the pond.

B

C

See - saw

D

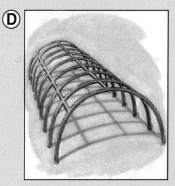

Tunnel

1 Write what the letters **N**, **E**, **S** and **W** stand for.
2 Name two things you could play on west of the pond.
3 Look at **C**. Which way is it from the pond?
4 Is **D** east or west of the pond?
5 Name the direction from the swings to the pond.
6 Can you make up a saying to help you remember the order of north, east, south and west using the first letters **N**, **E**, **S** and **W**?

Treasure Island
Aug 1750

Foremast Hill

North Inlet

ye Spye glass Hill

R Cove

N W E S

Spring forest

Swamp

Crams

Bulk of Treasure here

Swamp

Cape of ye Woods

White Rock

Mizzenmast Hill

Skeleton Island

Haulbowline Head

Foulground

Robert Louis Stevenson got the idea for his book, **Treasure Island**, when he drew a map of a treasure island. He thought it would make a good story. **E** is a map of the Treasure Island in his story. On his map of the island Robert Louis Stevenson included the **compass directions**, but he did not make a **key** for the map.

Look carefully at the map and work out what the shapes and colours show is on the island. He gave some of the places on his island names. He marked where the treasure was hidden.

1 Make a key for the Treasure Island map.
2 Which place on the island is named after a compass direction?
3 Which way is Spye glass Hill from the swamp?
4 Name the hill in the north of the island.
5 Which direction is it from the swamp to the spring?
6 If you landed at the end of North Inlet, which way would you go to find the treasure?
7 Which parts of the island do not have sandy beaches?

Directing the way

Look at the compass in **A**. It shows the four points of the compass. It also shows you four more compass directions, between north, east, south and west. Read what these are called.

We can use these directions to help find the way around the **picture map** of the park in **B**.

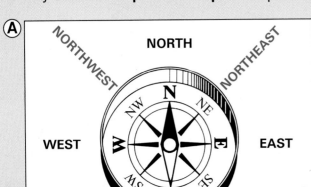

1 Which compass direction is it from North Gate to South Gate?
2 Is the lake in the northwest or the southwest of the park?
3 Which compass direction are the tennis courts from the fountain?
4 Follow these directions to find where to go:
   You are in the playground. Go north and turn west towards the football pitch. Then turn northwest. Turn southwest at the next turning. Then turn north.
   Which gate are you walking towards?
5 Say which way to go, using compass directions and turns, from the cafe to the toilets.

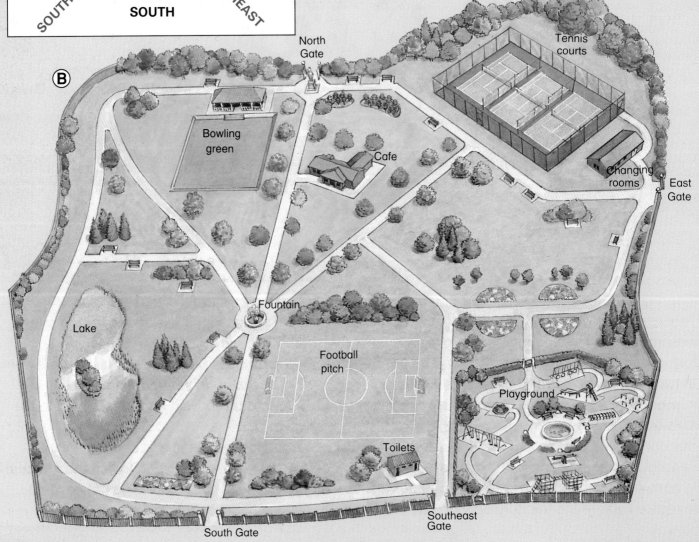

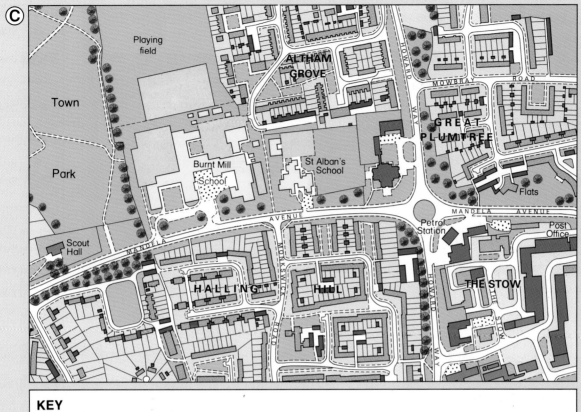

KEY

Homes	Church	School	Open space	• Trees
Garages and Sheds	Public buildings	Playground	Grass and Park	===== Road and Pavement
Shops	Factories and Offices	Car park	Gardens, walls and fences	===== Path

Map **C** shows the area around St. Alban's School. It shows what the buildings near the school are used for. The roads are named on the map.

Four areas in the neighbourhood are named also. One is Altham Grove. It is north of the school.

1 Which school is southwest of Altham Grove?

2 Which area is southeast of St. Alban's School?

3 Does Mandela Avenue go north-south or east-west?

4 Which compass direction is it from the Scout Hall to the Playing field?

5 Name the building northwest of the roundabout.

6 What is the name of the area southwest of Great Plumtree?

7 What are the buildings in the northeast of the area used for?

8 Find out where you would be going if you followed these instructions when you came out of St. Alban's School:
Turn east. Then turn south along the first road. Go east again along the next road. Where it turns north, go into the first building on the west side.
Name the roads you would have walked along and the type of building you went into.

9 Make up some journeys of your own. Use only compass directions to say which way to go.

Locating places

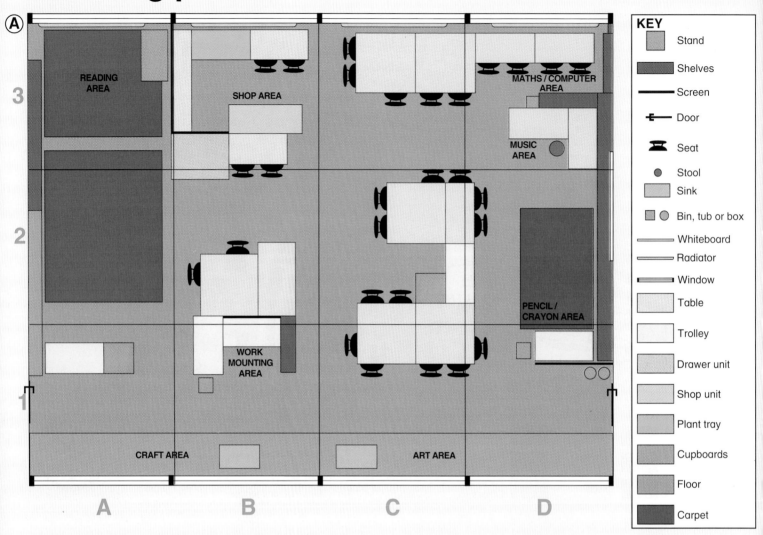

KEY

Stand	
Shelves	
Screen	
Door	
Seat	
Stool	
Sink	
Bin, tub or box	
Whiteboard	
Radiator	
Window	
Table	
Trolley	
Drawer unit	
Shop unit	
Plant tray	
Cupboards	
Floor	
Carpet	

A is a plan view of a classroom. Find the shop unit. It is next to a table, not far from a window and near the middle of the room. There are lots of tables near the middle of the room, and there are eight windows in the room. It is hard to say exactly where the shop unit is.

To help you be more exact, squares have been drawn on the vertical view. These squares make a **grid**. Letters have been written along the bottom of the grid. Numbers have been written up the side. **B** shows you how to use the letters and numbers to name a square in the grid.

To find the shop unit, put a finger on the letter **B** and a finger on the number **3**. Move your fingers up colomn **B** and across row **3** until they meet in the same square. This is **grid square** B3. You have found the shop unit. You can use the grid squares to say exactly where things are.

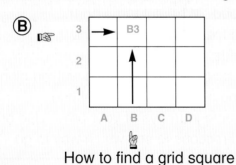

How to find a grid square

1 Using plan **A** name a feature in each of these grid squares:
       D3   A1   C2
2 Using plan **A** name a grid square which contains one of these:
       carpet   sink   bin

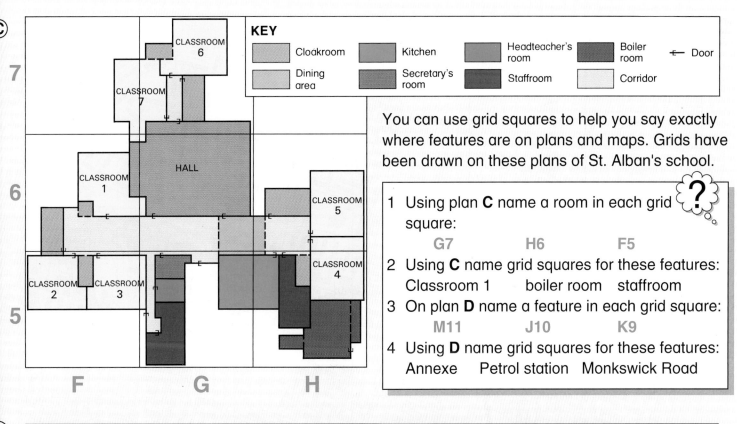

KEY

	Cloakroom		Kitchen		Headteacher's room		Boiler room
	Dining area		Secretary's room		Staffroom		Corridor

← Door

You can use grid squares to help you say exactly where features are on plans and maps. Grids have been drawn on these plans of St. Alban's school.

1 Using plan **C** name a room in each grid square:

    G7   H6   F5

2 Using **C** name grid squares for these features:
Classroom 1   boiler room   staffroom

3 On plan **D** name a feature in each grid square:

    M11   J10   K9

4 Using **D** name grid squares for these features:
Annexe   Petrol station Monkswick Road

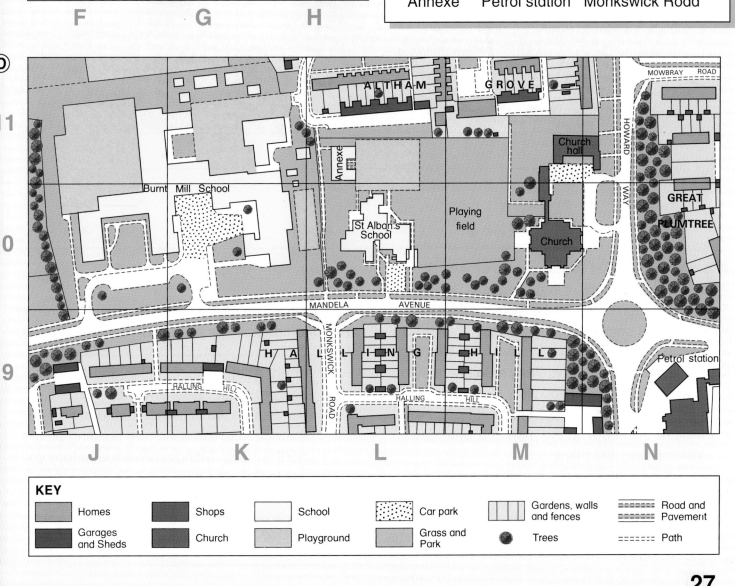

KEY

	Homes		Shops		School		Car park
	Garages and Sheds		Church		Playground		Grass and Park

	Gardens, walls and fences
●	Trees

═══	Road and Pavement
-----	Path

Street maps

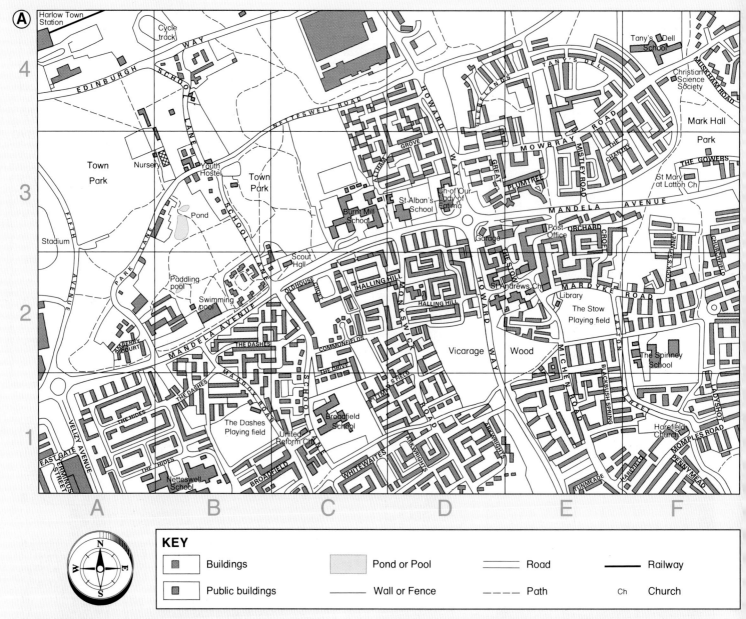

KEY

■ Buildings	▨ Pond or Pool	═══ Road	▬▬ Railway
■ Public buildings	─── Wall or Fence	- - - Path	Ch Church

A is a **street map** of the local area around St. Alban's School, which is in grid square **D3**. The street map names all the local roads. It also names some of the buildings.

It shows some other places in the local area.

Street maps are useful for finding the way around a local area. Use map **A** to find your way around.

1 In which grid square is Tany's Dell School?
2 Which roads would you walk along from Vicarage Wood, **D2**, to Mark Hall Park, **F4**?
3 Follow this route on the map and write down the missing directions:

   Start at the library in grid square **E2**.
   Go .... along Michen Road and turn .... onto the path south of Vicarage Wood. Turn .... into Howard Way and go north. At the roundabout in grid square .... turn west and pass two schools on the .... side of Mandela Avenue. Go to the named building on the north side of Mandela Avenue before you get to School Lane.
   Name the building and the grid square it is in.
4 Write the directions for a route of your own.

28

Index

A
Altham Grove C3
Amberry Court A2
Arkwrights D1

B
Blackbush Spring E1
Broadfield B1
Broadfield School C1
Burnt Mill School C3

C
Christian Science Society F4
Churchfield F3
Church of Our Lady of Fatima D3
Commonfields C2
Cook's Spinney F2
Cycle track B4

E
East Gate A1
Edinburgh Way A4

F
Fifth Avenue A3

G
Glebelands D4
Great Plumtree D3

H
Halling Hill C2, D2
Harefield F1
Harefield Church F1
Harlow Town Station A4
Howard Way D4, D2

L
Ladyshot F1
Latton Street E2
Library E2

M
Maddox Road B1
Mandela Avenue B2, E3
Mardyke Road E2
Mark Hall Park F4
Michen Road E2
Mistley Road E3
Monkswick Road D2
Momples Road F1
Mowbray Road E3
Muskham Road F4

N
Netteswell Road C4
Netteswell School B1
Nursery B3

O
Oldhouse Croft C2
Orchard Croft E3

P
Paddling pool B2
Park Lane A2
Pennymead F1
Petrol station D3
Pittman's Field C1
Pond B3
Post Office E3

S
School Lane B4, B3, C1
Scout Hall C2
Stadium A3
St Alban's School D3
St Andrews Church D2
St Mary at Latton Church F3
Swimming pool B2

T
Tany's Dell E4
Tany's Dell School F4
Terminus Street A1
The Chantry E3
The Dashes B1, B2
The Dashes Playing field B1
The Drive C2
The Gowers F3
The Hides A1, B1
The Spinney School F2
The Stow D2
The Stow Playing field E2
Town Park A3, B3
Tunmeade E1

U
United Reformed Church C1

V
Velizy Avenue A1
Vicarage Wood E1

W
Whitewaites C1

Y
Youth Hostel B3

All the names on street map **A** are listed in **B**. They are listed in **alphabetical order**. This is called an **index** to the street map. The index helps us find the places on the map.

One of the streets on the map is named Commonfields. Find Commenfields in the Index. Next to it is written the grid square it is in. This is called its **grid reference**. The grid reference for Commonfields is C2. Look at map **A** to find it.

1 Name a street that Commonfields joins on to.
2 Use the Index to help you find these streets on map **A**: Mistley Road   East Gate
   Name a street each one joins on to.
3 Find out whether these streets are north or south of St. Alban's School:
   Netteswell Road   Maddox Road
4 Make an index to show places you can visit in the local area. Include these places:
   Library E2   Youth Hostel B3

How far is it?

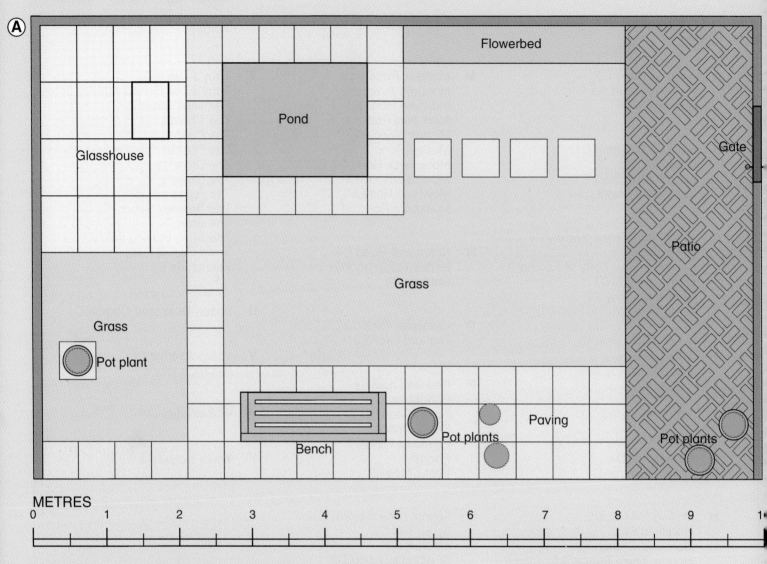

A

Flowerbed

Pond

Glasshouse

Gate

Patio

Grass

Grass

Pot plant

Bench

Pot plants

Paving

Pot plants

METRES

0 1 2 3 4 5 6 7 8 9 1

A is a plan view of a garden. It shows the garden much smaller than it really is. But how far is it from one end of the garden to the other?

You can use the **scale bar** to find out about the real **length** of the garden. You use it to **measure** distances. B and C show you how to use the scale bar to measure how long the bench is.

Lay the edge of a piece of paper along the bench. On the paper mark the length of the bench, like B. Now put the paper against the scale bar so that the first mark is under the 0 on the scale. Look at the scale to see where the second mark comes, like C. You can see that the real length of the bench is 2 metres.

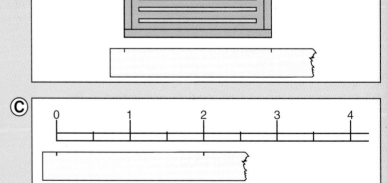

B

C

0 1 2 3 4

1 How long is the garden?
2 How wide is the garden?
3 How long is the flowerbed?
4 Which has the longest side: the glasshouse or the pond?

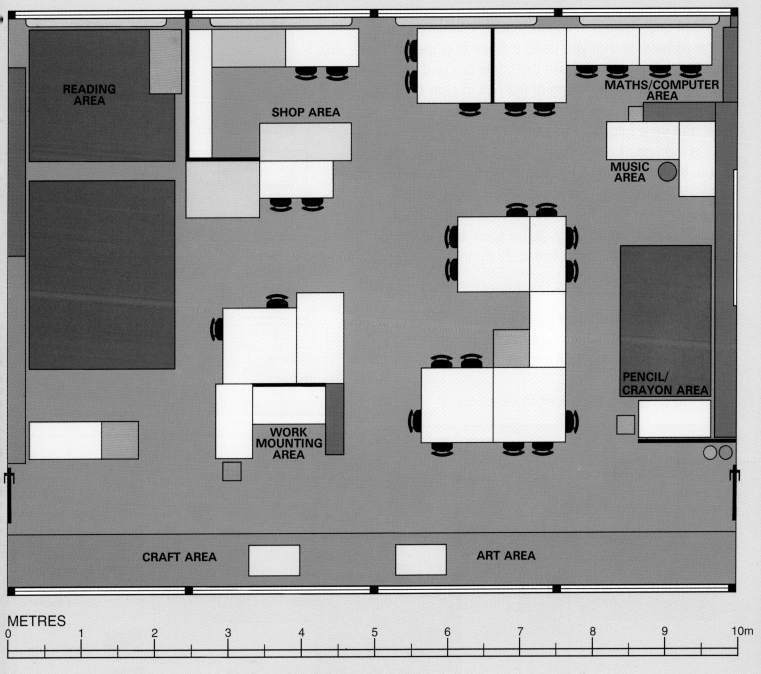

READING AREA

SHOP AREA

MATHS/COMPUTER AREA

MUSIC AREA

PENCIL/ CRAYON AREA

WORK MOUNTING AREA

CRAFT AREA

ART AREA

METRES

0   1   2   3   4   5   6   7   8   9   10m

D is a plan of a classroom. Use a piece of paper and the scale bar to help you measure distances and sizes in the classroom.

1 How long and wide is the classroom?
2 How long and wide are the narrow tables in the classroom?
3 How long and wide are the three carpets?
4 How far is it in a straight line from the left hand sink to the stool in the Music Area?

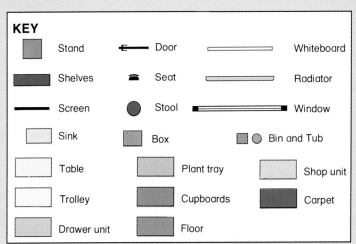

KEY

Stand	Door	Whiteboard
Shelves	Seat	Radiator
Screen	Stool	Window
Sink	Box	Bin and Tub
Table	Plant tray	Shop unit
Trolley	Cupboards	Carpet
Drawer unit	Floor	

Measuring on plans and maps

You can use a ruler to measure distances on plans, in the same way that you used a piece of paper. **A** and **B** show you how to use the scale bar and a ruler to measure the length of the hall in plan **C**.

First, put your ruler on the plan so the **0** is at one end of the hall. Look to see how many centimetres it is to the other end of the hall. In **A**, you can see it is 4 centimetres. To find the real length of the hall put your ruler along the scale bar, like **B**, and count along 4 centimetres. Look at the scale bar. It shows that the real length of the hall is 20 metres.

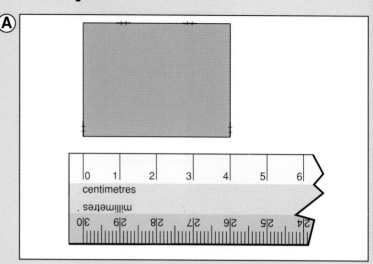

1 In a straight line, how far is it from class 5's door to class 8's door?
2 How wide are the hall and kitchen area together?
3 How long and wide is each classroom?

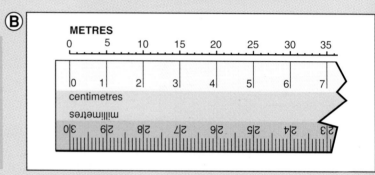

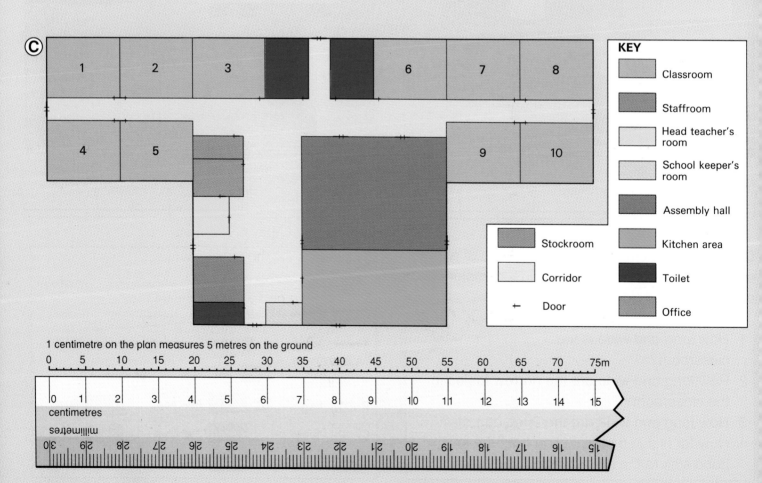

KEY

- Classroom
- Staffroom
- Head teacher's room
- School keeper's room
- Assembly hall
- Stockroom
- Corridor
- ← Door
- Kitchen area
- Toilet
- Office

1 centimetre on the plan measures 5 metres on the ground

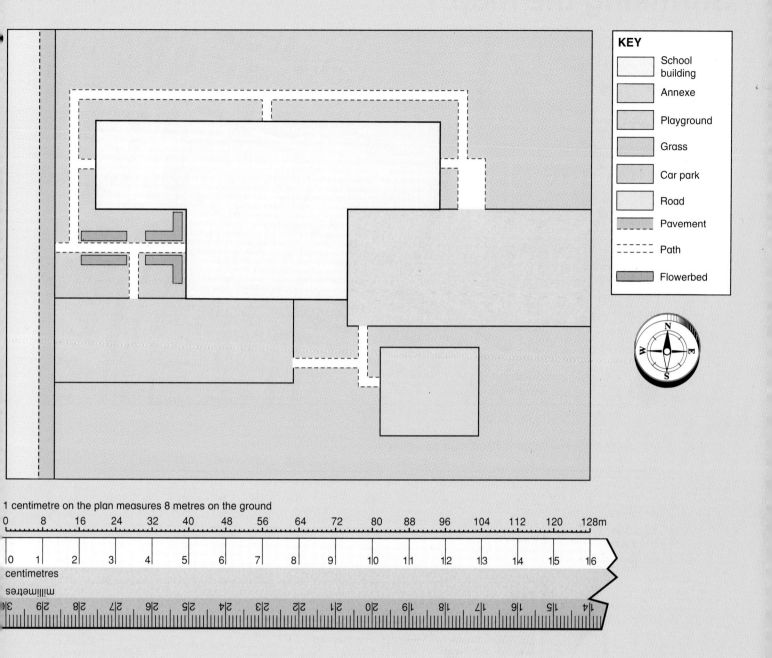

1 centimetre on the plan measures 8 metres on the ground

| 0 | 8 | 16 | 24 | 32 | 40 | 48 | 56 | 64 | 72 | 80 | 88 | 96 | 104 | 112 | 120 | 128m |

centimetres

millimetres

When a plan or map is drawn **accurately**, like **C** and **D**, so that you can measure distances on them, we say that they have been drawn to **scale**.

Below plan **C**, you can see that the scale bar shows that 1 centimetre on the ruler measures 5 metres of the real school building. This is the scale of the plan. It is written below plan **C**.

Plan **D** shows all the school grounds. It is drawn to a smaller scale than plan **C**, so that it can be fitted onto the page. Find the scale of plan **D**.

1 How long is the school building from east to west?
2 How long and wide is the school playground?
3 How long and wide are the school grounds?
4 How far is it along the path that goes from the pavement to the door by the headteacher's room?
5 What is the scale of plan **D**?

KEY

School building
Annexe
Playground
Grass
Car park
Road
Pavement
--- Path
Flowerbed

Shrinking the map 1

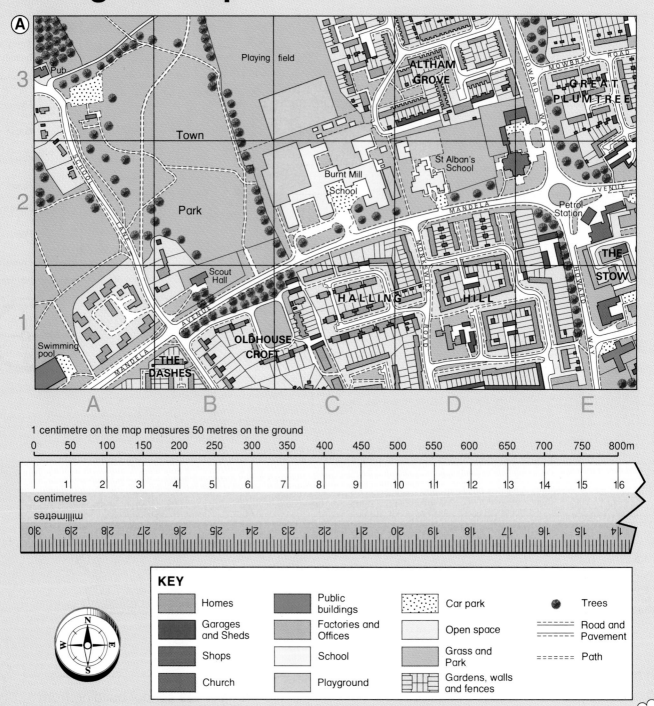

1 centimetre on the map measures 50 metres on the ground

KEY

Homes	Public buildings	Car park
Garages and Sheds	Factories and Offices	Open space
Shops	School	Grass and Park
Church	Playground	Gardens, walls and fences

Trees

Road and Pavement

Path

Look at map **A** of the area around St. Alban's School. The map has been drawn to scale. All the features have been drawn accurately. You can see their shapes and sizes clearly.
Find St. Alban's School. Its grid reference is **D2** Look at its shape. You can see all the corners of its walls.

1 Find the shapes in **B** on map **A**. Name each one.
2 How far is it from the roundabout to the Scout Hall along Mandela Avenue?
3 How far is it in a straight line from the pub in **A3** to the swimming pool in **A1**?
4 Find a grid square with six different features in it. Give its grid reference and name the features.

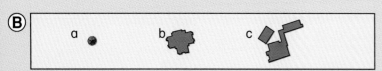

(B)
a   b   c

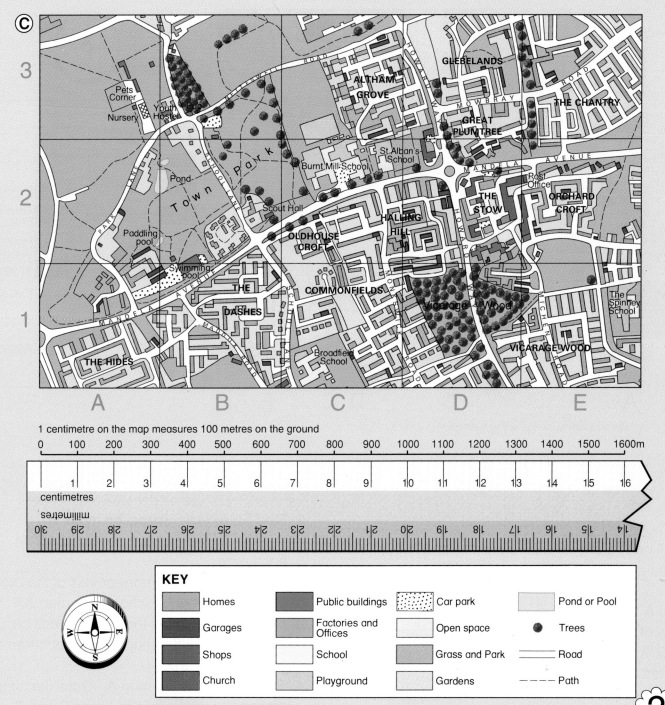

C

1 centimetre on the map measures 100 metres on the ground

| 0 | 100 | 200 | 300 | 400 | 500 | 600 | 700 | 800 | 900 | 1000 | 1100 | 1200 | 1300 | 1400 | 1500 | 1600m |

centimetres

millimetres

KEY

	Homes		Public buildings		Car park		Pond or Pool
	Garages		Factories and Offices		Open space	●	Trees
	Shops		School		Grass and Park	——	Road
	Church		Playground		Gardens	- - -	Path

Map **C** shows more of the local area around St. Alban's School. Everything on it has been drawn smaller so that more of the local area fits onto the page. Find St. Alban's School in grid square **C2** Its shape is roughly correct, but the map is too small to show all the corners and walls. This has happened to other features on the map too. The shapes and colours are still used to show what everything is. They are called **symbols**. The key shows what the symbols mean. You can use the scale bar to measure distances on the map.

1 Find the Scout Hall on maps **A** and **C**. Draw the symbol that shows it on each map.

2 What is the straight line distance from the Post Office in **E2** to the swimming pool in **B2**?

3 Why have all the trees around St. Alban's School not been drawn in? Compare the map with photo **F** on page 15.

35

Shrinking the map 2

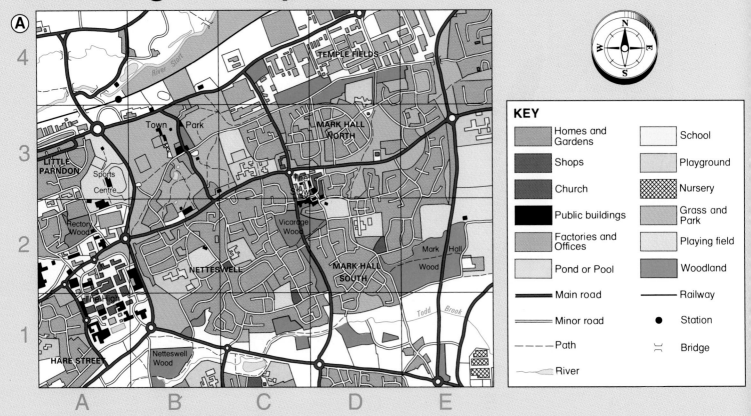

Ⓐ

KEY

Homes and Gardens		School	
Shops		Playground	
Church		Nursery	
Public buildings		Grass and Park	
Factories and Offices		Playing field	
Pond or Pool		Woodland	
——— Main road		——— Railway	
Minor road		● Station	
– – – Path		⊐⊏ Bridge	
River			

1 centimetre on the map measures 250 metres on the ground

Maps **A**, **B** and **C** show more of the area around St. Alban's School. Each map shows a larger area than you have seen before.

Map **A** shows the local area of the school in the town of Harlow. The school is in grid square **C3** On this map you can see the roads. But the homes and gardens are now shown only by a colour, not as buildings. Look in the key to see which colour symbol shows where people live.

Map **B** shows the whole of the town of Harlow. You can see that Harlow is to the west of the M11. The school is drawn so small that it is only just possible to see where it is in grid square **C3**

On map **C** the school is not even marked. The map shows that Harlow is near other towns. Use the key to see what the symbols mean.

36

?

1 Find St. Alban's School on maps **A** and **B**. Draw the shape of the school on each map.

2 Does map **B** show more or less of the area around St. Alban's School than map **A**?

3 Look for the symbol that shows trees on each map. Do the maps show each tree or just groups of trees?

4 Find Town Park on map **A**. Draw the shape that shows where it is on maps **B** and **C**.

5 Which map tells you that the River Stort is north of Harlow?

6 Name and write the grid references of four places on map **C** which the River Stort flows past.

7 The symbols on map **C** show how the land is used, but the colour white is not shown in the key. What do you think the colour white on the map means the land is used for?

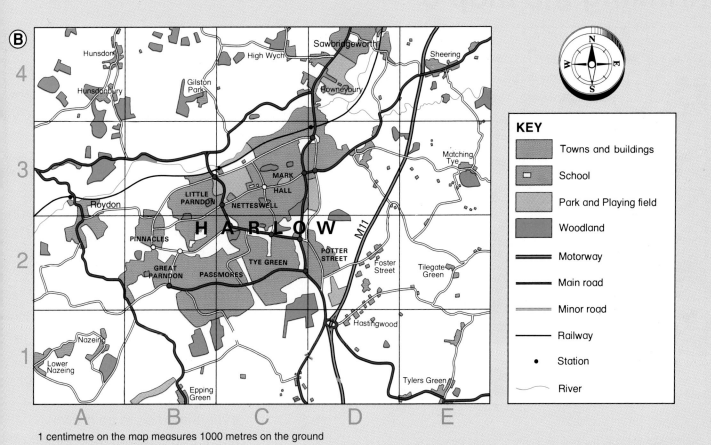

B

KEY

	Towns and buildings
	School
	Park and Playing field
	Woodland
	Motorway
	Main road
	Minor road
	Railway
•	Station
	River

1 centimetre on the map measures 1000 metres on the ground

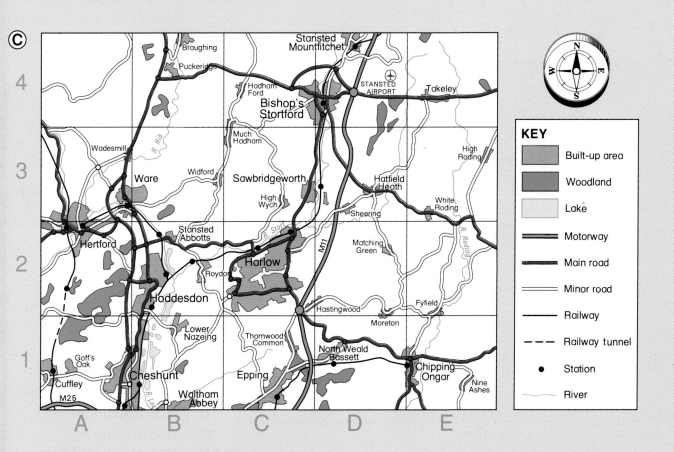

C

KEY

	Built-up area
	Woodland
	Lake
	Motorway
	Main road
	Minor road
	Railway
- - -	Railway tunnel
•	Station
	River

1 centimetre on the map measures 2500 metres on the ground

Shrinking the map 3

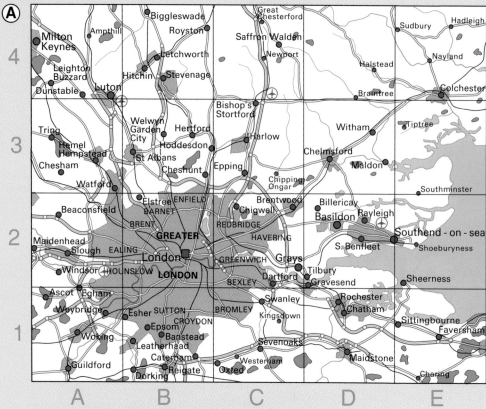

Ⓐ

1 centimetre on the map measures 10 kilometres on the ground

Maps **A** and **B** show where Harlow is.

Map **A** shows that Harlow is north of London. It is in grid square **C3**. This map shows the large towns and the main roads in the area around London.

On map **B** you can see that Harlow is in the southeast of England, in grid square **D3**.

On each map more and more of England is shown. Because everything has to be drawn smaller, many features are left off the map. They are too small to show. Only the largest towns in England and Wales are shown on map **B**, but only a few are named.

KEY

▨	Woodland	▦	Motorway
▨	Sea and Lakes	┄┄	Main road
		┄┄┄	Road tunnel
▨ ◾ •	Towns	—	Railway
⊕	Airport	◁═	River

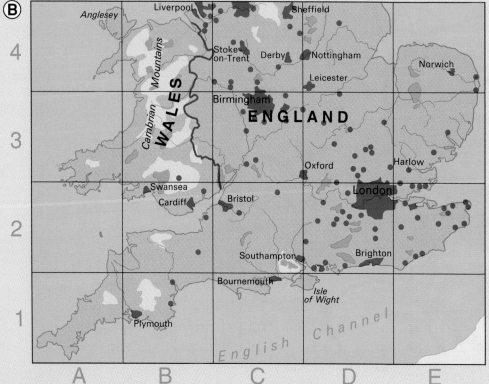

Ⓑ

1 centimetre on the map measures 40 kilometres on the ground

KEY

▨	Farmland	▨	Sea
▨	Moorland	🖤 •	Towns
▨	Forest and Woodland	—	River

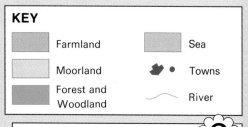

1. Draw how Harlow is shown on each map.
2. Name and give the grid squares of two towns southeast of London, on map **A**.
3. Make an index for the towns named in England and Wales on map **B**.
4. Farmland is shown on map **B**. Which colour includes farmland on map **A**?

©

C is a satellite photo of the British Isles.
On **C** find the part of the British Isles that you can see in map **B**.
The countries in the British Isles have been named on the photo. See what else is named.

1 Which country is north of England?
2 Which two towns are shown on **B** and **C**?
3 In which direction would you sail from Wales to Northern Ireland?

Mapping the British Isles

A

KEY

High land

Low land

River

National boundary

■ Capital city

• Other city

7 Orkney Islands

9 Shetland Islands

6

8

Northwest Highlands

Grampian Mountains

SCOTLAND

• Glasgow   ■ Edinburgh

ATLANTIC OCEAN

Southern Uplands

NORTH SEA

NORTHERN IRELAND

■ Belfast

Lake District

The Pennines

U   N   I   T   E   D

REPUBLIC

OF

IRELAND

IRISH SEA

• Dublin

Liverpool • • Manchester

Snowdonia

K   I   N   G   D   O   M

Trent

• Birmingham

Severn

ENGLAND

WALES

Thames

Cardiff ■

■ London

1 centimetre on the map measures
40 kilometres on the ground

ENGLISH CHANNEL

© Collins ◇ Longman Atlases

1 **A**   **B**   **C**   **D**   **E**   **F**

A is a map of the British Isles. The symbols in the key tell you what the shapes, lines and colours on the map mean. Photos **B** to **F** also show you what the symbols mean.

On map **A** some of the rivers and areas of high land are named. The countries are named and so are their capital cities.
Some other cities are named too.

1 Find Scotland on map **A**. Name two high land areas in Scotland.
2 Find Wales on map **A**. What is the name of the capital city of Wales?
3 Use maps **G** and **A** to work out which part of the United Kingdom is in the island of Ireland?
4 Name two rivers in England.

High land

Ⓒ Low land

Ⓓ River

National boundary

Ⓕ ▪ Capital city

Ⓖ

REPUBLIC OF IRELAND   UNITED KINGDOM

British Isles - towns index

Thurso
Wick
Stornoway
Lewis
Harris
Ullapool
North Uist
Elgin
Fraserburgh
Inverness
South Uist
Portree
Skye
Aberdeen
Rhum
Mallaig
Fort William
SCOTLAND
Dundee
Mull
Oban
Perth
Stirling
Kirkcaldy
Jura
Greenock
Edinburgh
Berwick
Islay
Glasgow
Kilmarnock
Arran
Selkirk
Ayr
Hawick
Campbeltown
Londonderry
Larne
Stranraer
Dumfries
Newcastle
NORTHERN IRELAND
Bangor
Carlisle
Sunderland
Belfast
Workington
Durham
Middlesbrough
Sligo
Darlington
Scarborough
Isle of Man
Barrow-in-Furness
Lancaster
York
Douglas
Westport
REPUBLIC
Blackpool
Bradford
Hull
Preston
Leeds
Grimsby
Drogheda
Manchester
Doncaster
Galway
Athlone
OF
Liverpool
Sheffield
Lincoln
Dublin
Holyhead
Anglesey
IRELAND
Wicklow
Colwyn Bay
Chester
ENGLAND
Limerick
Crewe
Nottingham
Stoke
Derby
Norwich
Stafford
Great Yarmouth
Tralee
Telford
Leicester
Peterborough
Waterford
Aberystwyth
Birmingham
Ipswich
Killarney
Cork
Wexford
Coventry
Cambridge
Harwich
Worcester
Northampton
Colchester
Fishguard
WALES
Milton Keynes
Harlow
Milford Haven
Merthyr Tydfil
Hereford
Oxford
Southend
Swansea
Gloucester
London
Margate
Newport
Swindon
Reading
Canterbury
Cardiff
Bristol
Bath
Maidstone
Dover
Folkestone
Barnstaple
Salisbury
Hastings
Taunton
Southampton
Brighton
Bournemouth
Portsmouth
Exeter
Cowes
Weymouth
Isle of Wight
Torbay
Plymouth
Isles of Scilly
Penzance

Shetland Islands
Lerwick
Orkney Islands
Kirkwall
Thurso
Wick

© Collins ◇ Longman Atlases

Map **A** shows some of the towns in each part
of the British Isles.
Each town is shown by a dot, like this: •
This **symbol** shows where the town is. The name
of the town is written next to it. The town of York is
shown on the map like this:

• York

If we want to find where a town is on the map,
we can use the **Index** to help us. **B** is the Index
for map **A**. Find Cork in the Index in **B**.
The Index shows it is in grid square **B3**.
Find grid reference **B3** on the map.

1 Use the Index in **B** to find:
   London Cardiff Edinburgh Belfast
2 Use the Index to help you find where
   some other towns are on the map. Start
   with Stirling.
3 Is your home near or in one of the towns
   on the map? What is its grid reference?
4 Choose a map on another page, which has
   grid squares over it. Make an Index for
   the map.

Index

A Aberdeen **F9**
Aberystwyth **E3**
Athlone **B5**
Ayr **D7**

B Bangor **D6**
Barnstaple **E2**
Barrow-in-Furness **E5**
Bath **F2**
Belfast **D6**
Berwick **F7**
Birmingham **F4**
Blackpool **E5**
Bournemouth **F2**
Bradford **F5**
Brighton **G2**
Bristol **F2**

C Cambridge **G3**
Campbeltown **D7**
Canterbury **H2**
Cardiff **E3**
Carlisle **E6**
Chester **E4**
Colchester **H3**
Colwyn Bay **E4**
Cork **B3**
Coventry **F4**
Cowes **G2**
Crewe **F4**

D Darlington **F6**
Derby **F4**
Doncaster **G5**
Douglas **D5**
Dover **H2**
Drogheda **C5**

Dublin **C5**
Dumfries **E6**
Dundee **E8**
Durham **F6**

E Edinburgh **E7**
Elgin **E9**
Exeter **E2**

F Fishguard **D3**
Folkestone **H2**
Fort William **D8**
Fraserburgh **F9**

G Galway **B5**
Glasgow **E7**
Gloucester **F3**
Great Yarmouth **H4**
Greenock **D7**
Grimsby **G5**

H Harlow **H3**
Harwich **H3**
Hastings **H2**
Hawick **F7**
Hereford **F3**
Holyhead **D5**
Hull **G5**

I Inverness **E9**
Ipswich **H3**

K Killarney **A3**
Kilmarnock **D7**
Kirkcaldy **E8**
Kirkwall **E11**

L Lancaster **F5**
Larne **D6**
Leeds **F5**
Leicester **G4**
Lerwick **F12**
Limerick **B4**
Lincoln **G5**
Liverpool **E5**
London **G3**
Londonderry **C6**

M Maidstone **H2**
Mallaig **D9**
Manchester **F5**
Margate **H3**
Merthyr Tydfil **E3**
Middlesbrough **F6**
Milford Haven **D3**
Milton Keynes **G3**

N Newcastle **F6**
Newport **E3**
Northampton **G3**
Norwich **H4**
Nottingham **G4**

O Oban **D8**
Oxford **G3**

P Penzance **D1**
Perth **E8**
Peterborough **G4**
Plymouth **E1**
Portree **C9**
Portsmouth **G2**
Preston **F5**

R Reading **G3**

S Salisbury **F2**
Scarborough **G6**
Selkirk **E7**
Sheffield **F5**
Sligo **B6**
Southampton **G2**
Southend **H3**
Stafford **F4**
Stirling **E8**
Stoke **F4**
Stornoway **C10**
Stranraer **D6**
Sunderland **F6**
Swansea **E3**
Swindon **F3**

T Taunton **E2**
Telford **F4**
Thurso **E10**
Torbay **E1**
Tralee **A4**

U Ullapool **D10**

W Waterford **C3**
Westport **A5**
Wexford **C3**
Weymouth **F2**
Wick **E10**
Wicklow **C4**
Worcester **F3**
Workington **E6**

Y York **G5**

Europe

A is a satellite photo of part of Europe. Find the land and the sea. Some of the mountains and rivers have been named on **A**. It also shows the seas around Europe.

You can see the whole of Europe in map **B**. If you watch or listen to the news, you will often hear the names of countries in Europe.
Map **B** shows where each country is and which countries are neighbours. Some countries have many neighbours; others have few.

The colours on map **B** show the shape of each country. The red lines on the map show the borders of each country.

1 Which ocean is north of Europe?
2 Which countries have only one neighbour?
3 Which country has most neighbours?
4 How many countries are there in Europe?
5 Name the country both France and Portugal have a border with.
6 Name the country which has Germany, Austria, Italy and France around it.
7 Find the Alps in **A**. Name a country on **B** where you could visit the Alps.
8 Which is the most eastern country in Europe?
9 Listen to the news on the radio or TV. Make a list of how many times European countries are mentioned. Find them on a map of Europe.

KEY
- ■ Capital city
- • Other town or city
- — Country boundary

1 centimetre on the map measures
200 kilometres on the ground

ARCTIC
OCEAN

ATLANTIC

OCEAN

Reykjavik ■ ICELAND

North

Sea

N O R W A Y

S W E D E N

FINLAND
Helsinki ■
• St. Petersburg
Oslo ■
Tallinn ■
Stockholm ■
ESTONIA
RUSSIAN
FEDERATION
■ Moscow
LATVIA
■ Riga
LITHUANIA
Vilnius ■
R.F.
■ Minsk
BELORUSSIA

Edinburgh •
DENMARK
Copenhagen ■

IRELAND
Dublin •
UNITED
KINGDOM
London ■
NETHERLANDS
Hamburg •
Amsterdam •
Berlin ■
GERMANY
Warsaw ■
POLAND
• Kiev
UKRAINE
Brussels ■
BELGIUM
• Bonn
LUXEMBOURG
Prague ■
CZECH
REPUBLIC
SLOVAKIA
Paris ■
Munich •
Vienna ■
Bratislava ■
MOLDAVIA
■ Kishinev
FRANCE
Berne ■
AUSTRIA
Budapest ■
SWITZERLAND
HUNGARY
ROMANIA
Lyon •
Ljubljana ■
Turin •
SLOVENIA
Zagreb ■
CROATIA
Belgrade ■
Bucharest ■
Black
Sea
Oporto •
ANDORRA
Marseille •
BOSNIA-
HERZEGOVINA
Sarajevo •
YUGO-
SLAVIA
BULGARIA
PORTUGAL
Madrid •
Barcelona •
Rome ■
ITALY
Sofia ■
Lisbon ■
SPAIN
ALBANIA
Tiranë ■
Skopje ■
MACEDONIA
Istanbul •
TURKEY
Naples •
ASIA
Gibraltar
(U.K.)
GREECE
Athens •
Mediterranean
Sea
AFRICA
MALTA

45

The World

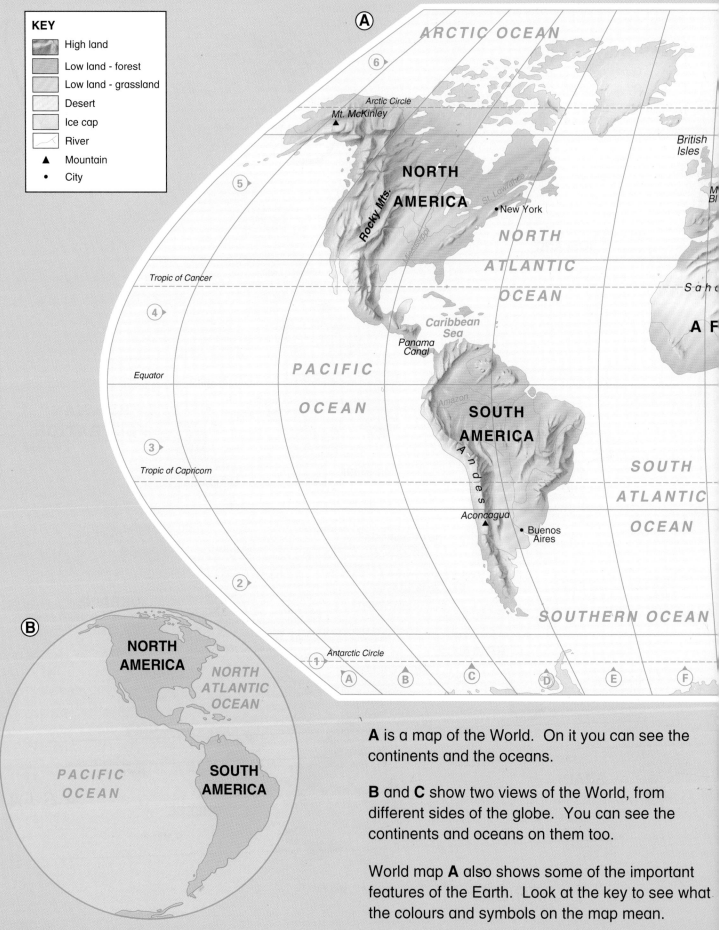

KEY

▨	High land
▨	Low land - forest
▢	Low land - grassland
▢	Desert
▢	Ice cap
⌇	River
▲	Mountain
•	City

ARCTIC OCEAN

Arctic Circle

Mt. McKinley

NORTH AMERICA

Rocky Mts.

St. Lawrence

• New York

NORTH ATLANTIC OCEAN

British Isles

Tropic of Cancer

Mississippi

Caribbean Sea

Panama Canal

Sah

A F

Equator

PACIFIC OCEAN

Amazon

SOUTH AMERICA

Andes

SOUTH ATLANTIC OCEAN

Tropic of Capricorn

Aconcagua

• Buenos Aires

Antarctic Circle

SOUTHERN OCEAN

NORTH AMERICA

NORTH ATLANTIC OCEAN

PACIFIC OCEAN

SOUTH AMERICA

A is a map of the World. On it you can see the continents and the oceans.

B and **C** show two views of the World, from different sides of the globe. You can see the continents and oceans on them too.

World map **A** also shows some of the important features of the Earth. Look at the key to see what the colours and symbols on the map mean.

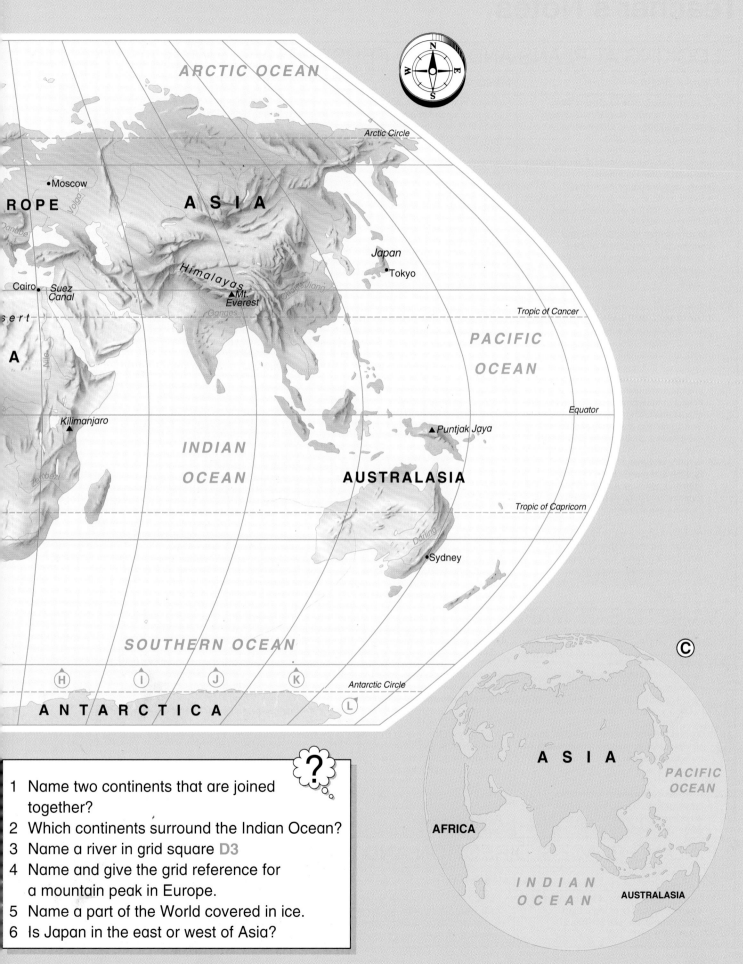

ARCTIC OCEAN

Arctic Circle

• Moscow

EUROPE

ASIA

Japan
• Tokyo

Cairo • Suez Canal

▲ Mt. Everest

Himalayas

Ganges

Tropic of Cancer

PACIFIC

OCEAN

Kilimanjaro
▲

INDIAN

OCEAN

▲ Puntjak Jaya

Equator

AUSTRALASIA

Tropic of Capricorn

Darling

• Sydney

SOUTHERN OCEAN

Ⓗ   Ⓘ   Ⓙ   Ⓚ

Antarctic Circle

Ⓛ

ANTARCTICA

ⓒ

ASIA

PACIFIC
OCEAN

AFRICA

INDIAN
OCEAN

AUSTRALASIA

1 Name two continents that are joined together?
2 Which continents surround the Indian Ocean?
3 Name a river in grid square **D3**
4 Name and give the grid reference for a mountain peak in Europe.
5 Name a part of the World covered in ice.
6 Is Japan in the east or west of Asia?

Teacher's Notes

LOOKING AT PLANS AND MAPS: PERSPECTIVE, SYMBOLS AND KEY

Ideas / Skills	Resources	Extension Activities	Nat Cur Geo POS Links
2-3 Draw round objects to make a plan. • the view from above: plan and shape • identifying objects in plan view • vocabulary: shape, plan	• objects to look straight down on • photos of objects in plan • plans of objects for children to identify • toys, overhead projector (OHP)	• draw plans of objects for others to identify • match plans to pictures • project shape of toy onto screen by placing toy on OHP, draw round toy, remove toy, leave plan	KS2 / 3c KS2 / 3d
4-5 Identify features on vertical aerial photos and match them to a map. **Interpret symbols using maps.** • terms: 'oblique view' and 'vertical view' • matching oblique and vertical views	• school area oblique and vertical photos and large scale map eg 1:1250 or 1:2500 scale • aerial photos and large scale maps of other localities	• discuss what can be seen in the photos • find features on oblique and vertical aerial photos • look at how features are shown on the local map • compare the map symbols to the feature shapes on the vertical aerial photo	KS2 / 3c KS2 / 3d KS2 / 3e
6-7 Identify British Isles, Europe and continents on maps and globes. • satellite and space photos • identifying shapes of areas on photos and maps	• satellite/space photos of Earth • inflatable globes and globe on stand • maps of continents and Earth • cut-out shapes of continents and other large areas of the Earth, eg islands	• match satellite photo of continents with shapes of the continents on map/globe • pass inflatable globe around the class/group, call out the name of a continent/ocean/island, child to find, then pass on	KS2 / 3d KS2 / 3d
8-9 Interpret symbols using maps. **Identify features from vertical viewpoints and match them to a map.** • plan as showing layout and shape of features and names	• photos of part of classroom • plans of room: acurate/with errors • cue cards for: location, direction, size and distance	• children draw own plan of room • give children plan of room which includes errors, for children to identify and correct • use cue cards for finding features in, and routes around, the room and plans of it • use features and plan to orient plan correctly	KS2 / 3c KS2 / 3d
10-11 Interpret symbols using maps. **Follow routes and describe the location of features using maps.** • relating oblique and aerial photos • use of colour code for categories of use	• oblique/vertical photos of school • plans of school building • base maps of the rooms in school • simple verbal (taped/written) directions to follow routes around school	• discuss where rooms are in school and how to get to them • make a survey of room use in school, make a colour coded school use map, create a key • give directions for drawing routes on a base map	KS2 / 2b KS2 / 3d KS2 / 3e
12-13 Identify features on vertical aerial photos and match them to a map. **Interpret symbols and describe the location of places using maps.** • showing larger area in the same space	• photos of school and grounds from a variety of angles • map of school and grounds • copy of the large scale OS map of the school:1:1250 or 1:2500 scale	• find where ground level photos were taken, match in situ and on map; mark where taken on map • mark routes on a map of the school grounds • use a base map of the school grounds, survey the use of land, colour code and create key	KS2 / 3c KS2 / 3d KS2 / 3e KS2 / 5a
14-15 Identify features on vertical aerial photos and match them to a map. **Interpret symbols, follow routes and locate places using maps.** • as more of an area is shown, everything is drawn smaller	• photos of features in local area • oblique and vertical aerial photos • OS maps of the local area: 1:1250 or 1:2500 scale and 1:10 000 scale • photos of local road signs • plan shapes of individual features	• match oblique and vertical photos and ground level photos with local area maps • locate street signs on local map, using sign and background information in photo; go out to find some near school • find shapes on photos and map, identify features	KS2 / 3d KS2 / 3e KS2 / 5a

VARIETIES OF MAPS

Ideas / Skills	Resources	Extension Activities	Nat Cur Geo POS Links
16-17 Make maps of routes. **Make sketch maps of small areas showing the main features and using symbols with a key.** • drawing a map for a purpose, map/selective	• photos of features around local area • vertical photo and large scale OS and street maps of local area • teacher drawn maps of different parts of local area	• children to draw maps from school/home to local facilities, eg park, shops, garage, etc. • check accuracy of map against OS/street maps • give children photos of known local landmarks and ask them to draw map to show where they are	KS2 / 2b KS2 / 3c KS2 / 5a
18-19 Extract information from pictorial maps. **Use pictures to identify features and find out about places.** • use of a familiar story for mapwork	• copy of Fantastic Mr. Fox (Roald Dahl) • other stories in which there are pictures/maps of human and physical landscapes/environments	• Read Fantastic Mr. Fox and encourage use of the map during the story • encourage children to make their own maps of the areas in which they set their stories	KS2 / 3d KS2 / 5a
20-21 Maps as a sources of information. • develops idea of a variety of maps • ways information can be shown on maps • maps for particular purposes	• copies of a variety of maps, eg from adverts, postcards, newspapers, tourist brochures, magazines. • photos of maps seen in the local area	• discuss what maps show, who might use them, usefulness, if they could be better drawn • make keys for maps without keys • compare maps of different types of the local area	KS2 / 3d KS2 / 5a

FINDING PLACES: DIRECTION AND LOCATION

Ideas / Skills	Resources	Extension Activities	Nat Cur Geo POS Links
22-23 Use the eight points of the compass. **Interpret symbols using a map.** **Identify land and sea on maps.** • vocabulary: north, east, south, west	• transparent compass rose showing north, east, south, west, as an overlay • compasses, large for demonstration and small for personal use	• use compass to find out direction N, E, S and W in classroom and playground (explore effect of iron) and mark on classroom/school walls • use overlay on playground/treasure island maps	KS2 / 3d